# PLAIN
## LANGUAGE
### CLEAR AND SIMPLE

Une publication française sur le langage clair et simple a également été publiée. Cette publication est intitulée *Pour un style clair et simple*

© Minister of Supply and Services Canada 1991
Available in Canada through
Associated Bookstores
and other booksellers
or by mail from
Canada Communication Group – Publishing
Ottawa, Canada K1A 0S9
Catalogue No. Ci53-3/3-1991E
ISBN 0-660-14185-X

This publication is available in print, in braille and on audio cassette.

# PARTNERS

In completing this project, NGL Consulting Ltd. and the National Literacy Secretariat of the Department of Multiculturalism and Citizenship Canada depended on the advice and support of a working group of people from the following federal government departments:

- Consumer and Corporate Affairs
- Employment and Immigration
- Health and Welfare
- Industry, Science and Technology
- Justice
- National Library
- Privy Council Office
- Revenue Canada Taxation
- Secretary of State
- Seniors Secretariat
- Supply and Services
- Transport Canada
- Treasury Board
- Veterans Affairs

Their enthusiasm for the issue and the project helped make this guide a reality.

A special thank you to those who helped field test a draft version of this guide. Their thoughtful feedback helped make sure that this guide meets the needs of its readers.

# TABLE OF CONTENTS

Page

1.  **Plain Language and the Public Servant** ......................1
    How to Use This Guide ...................................2
    What Is Plain Language Writing? ..........................3
    Why Is Plain Language Important?..........................4

2.  **Before You Start Writing**.........................6
    Who Is Your Audience?...................................6
    Why Are You Writing This Document? ......................7
    What Do You Want to Say?................................7
    How Will Your Reader Use the Information in This Document? .....8
    How Should You Organize the Information? ..................8
    How Should You Present the Information? ...................9

3.  **Make Your Writing Effective**................................10
    Organize Your Ideas....................................10
    Help Your Reader Find Important Information ...............11
    Write the Way You Speak ...............................11
    Address Your Readers Directly ...........................12

4.  **Clear and Simple — Paragraphs and Sentences**..........15
    Limit Each Paragraph to One Idea ........................15
    Don't Overload Sentences ..............................17
    Active Sentences.......................................18
    Keep It Short .........................................20
    Keep It Simple ........................................21
    Link Your Ideas .......................................23
    Avoid Ambiguity ......................................23
    Emphasize the Positive..................................24
    Avoid Double Negatives ................................25

**5.   Think about Your Choice of Words**...........................**27**
Use Simple, Everyday Words ............................27
Cut Out Unnecessary Words ............................28
Avoid Using Jargon ....................................29
Avoid or Explain Technical Words ......................31
Don't Change Verbs into Nouns .........................32
Avoid Chains of Nouns .................................33
Explain Complex Ideas..................................34
Choose Your Words Carefully ...........................35
Use Acronyms Carefully ................................35

**6.   Appearances Are Very Important**...........................**37**
Spacing ...............................................37
Headings and Sub-Headings.............................39
Highlighting...........................................39
Table of Contents .....................................40
Type Style and Size ...................................40
Colour of Ink and Paper...............................42
Graphics and Illustrations ............................42

**7.   Check with the Experts — Your Readers**..................**44**

**8.   A Check List**.........................................**46**

**9.   For More Information** .................................**48**

# 1. Plain Language and the Public Servant

As a public servant, you are probably more aware than most people that we are living in an information age. In fact, you may sometimes feel overwhelmed by memos, letters, directives, manuals, brochures, reports and policy papers.

In your work, you may also have to write many documents. And the words you write may reach beyond the public service to Canadians across the country and abroad.

People with a wide range of reading abilities should be able to understand written messages from public servants and government departments. All Canadians are affected by government regulations and programs in many different but important ways. Whether they need to know about conservation, tax matters or radon gas levels in their homes, and whether they are excellent readers or not, Canadians have a right to receive clear information from the federal government.

Like other Canadians, public servants are sometimes subjected to writing that is filled with official-sounding jargon, or bureaucratese. You may feel frustrated by information that affects your work that is written in ways only an expert on the subject can understand.

Have you ever found yourself:

- re-reading sentences and paragraphs in reports, memos or manuals to try to understand them,

- not reading a document if you don't have to, because it seems too technical, complex or wordy,

- wondering if what you have written is clear, but concluding that it must be, because everyone writes about the subject that way?

Unclear writing can lead to misunderstandings, errors and wasted time. You can use the principles and tips in this guide to make sure that *your* writing is clear, concise and well-organized.

This guide shows how you can make even complex subjects easy to understand by using plain language techniques. You can use these techniques to transform rambling, intimidating prose into interesting, to-the-point writing. You can also organize your information in ways that get your message across most effectively.

# How to Use This Guide

This guide is designed to help you with each step as you write. From organizing your ideas to deciding on how your finished document should look, these techniques will help you communicate clearly and effectively.

This first chapter defines plain language writing and explains its importance in making government documents understandable. You can use plain language to reach Canadians with varying literacy skills. Chapter 2, **Before You Start Writing**, presents a series of questions about your reading audience and your purpose in writing the document that will help you as you draft your text. Chapter 3, **Make Your Writing Effective**, suggests ways to structure your document and recommends using a personal tone in your writing.

Chapter 4, **Clear and Simple — Paragraphs and Sentences**, advocates writing in a straightforward, active, positive way. Chapter 5, **Think about Your Choice of Words**, reminds you to use words that are familiar to your reader and to make sure that you meet your reader's need for information and explanations.

Once you have completed your document, you can use the advice in Chapter 6, **Appearances Are Important Too**, to present and highlight your information in ways that make your document easy to read. Chapter 7, **Check with the Experts — Your Readers**, offers pointers on testing the readability of your document with the people for whom you wrote it. The **Check List** that follows in Chapter 8 will help you gauge your success in writing plainly. The guide closes with a listing of sources you can refer to **For More Information**.

# What Is Plain Language Writing?

Plain language writing is a technique of organizing information in ways that make sense to the reader. It uses straightforward, concrete, familiar words. You can use these techniques to adapt what you have to say to the reading abilities of the people who are likely to read your document. Using plain language to explain concepts and procedures involves using examples that relate to your reader's experience.

Some government documents may be written for readers with specialized knowledge, such as scientists, lawyers or corporate executives. But other documents, about applying for a Social Insurance Number or family allowance, for example, are meant for Canadians who may not have background knowledge of the subject. All types of government writing can benefit from applying plain language techniques. Even technical and specialized texts can be improved with plain language techniques.

# Why Is Plain Language Important?

Plain language writing can save you time. By writing in ways that make government policies and procedures clearer, you will spend less time correcting errors and responding to people who didn't understand what you were trying to say.

Plain language also helps you reach the many Canadians who cannot read well. These readers have a right to government information that is written simply and presented clearly.

In 1990, Statistics Canada published the results of a survey on Canadians' literacy skills. The researchers found that more than one in three Canadian adults have some difficulty with everyday reading tasks. One in six Canadians cannot determine how much medicine to give a child by looking at the bottle label. More than one in five have trouble interpreting a line graph or filling out a catalogue order form.

While many Canadians have trouble with everyday reading material, even more find government information difficult to understand. Three out of five Canadians responding to a 1990 Decima Research study said they had trouble with government forms. More than three-quarters of Canadians think that all government documents should be written more clearly!

## PLAIN LANGUAGE WRITING:

- reaches people who cannot read well

- helps all readers understand information

- avoids misunderstandings and errors

- saves time, because it gets the job done well the first time

# 2. Before You Start Writing

Plain language writing focuses on the needs of the **reader**. Instead of cramming in every bit of information the writer wants to share, the plain writer considers:

- what needs the reader has,
- what information is essential, and
- how it can be organized and expressed most clearly.

To determine this, you can ask yourself a series of questions which will help you focus your writing and get your message across most effectively. Getting the answers to these questions may take a little bit of research, but the time you spend planning what you write will save you time and trouble later.

## Who Is Your Audience?

Are you writing *only* for professionals? Is your document intended for young people, seniors, working Canadians, public servants or members of specific ethnocultural groups? What do you know about the reading skills and backgrounds of the people who will use your document? Is English or French their second language? Are their reading skills likely to be uniformly high or low, or to vary? If even a few of your readers are likely to have low reading skills, you should write in a way that makes most of what you are saying understandable to them.

Consider the particular needs of readers with disabilities. Print is not appropriate for all audiences. You should think about using alternate media for your message, such as audio tapes, braille, large print and open and closed captioning for video material.

# Why Are You Writing This Document?

Are you writing about something completely new? Give your reader all the background information needed to understand the purpose of your new program or policy. Try to link the new information to things your reader may already know.

Are you trying to change people's behaviour? Make sure you mention how even small changes can bring benefits that are important to your reader.

Is your document a "how-to" text? Be sure to include any background information your reader may need to understand your instructions.

# What Do You Want to Say?

Focus on what your reader wants and needs to know. Don't try to say more about your subject than you have to. You will have to include information such as eligibility criteria and deadline dates. You may have to include information such as the history of government activity in the subject area. But if you can leave out some less important information, do so. Make sure that your reader's needs and wants determine what information gets the most emphasis. This information should go at the beginning or get the most attention in your document.

# How Will Your Reader Use the Information in This Document?

Will your document be a quick reference tool that your reader will use on the job? Will your reader find your document in a display, skim it to see if there is anything of particular interest and then read only one or two sections? Will your reader want or need to read it through to get a thorough understanding of the subject? How people use your document will help you decide how to organize the information in it.

# How Should You Organize the Information?

What does your reader most want to know? What is your main message or theme? Decide what information must be included and what can be left out. Then divide your information into main and secondary points.

Develop a structure for your document that will make it easy and enjoyable to use. Chronological order might be the most logical approach for describing procedures — step-by-step instructions, for example — or a sequence of events.

If people already know something about the subject and you are sharing new information, start with the old information, then introduce the new. If it's a new way of doing something familiar, describe the old procedure briefly before explaining the new steps.

If you are describing something completely new, start with general information about the program objectives or the reason for the policy, then deal with the specifics, such as the application procedures or rules.

# How Should You Present the Information?

To decide on your document's format, ask yourself if your reading audience has any special needs. Should your document be multilingual? Should it use large print, drawings or photographs? Should it be a pamphlet, booklet or book? Should it be portable or will it stay on a bookshelf for quick reference in an office?

Your answers to these questions will help you keep on track as you write and will ensure that your finished document meets your needs and those of your reader.

---

**BEFORE YOU START WRITING, ask yourself:**

- Who is your audience?

- Why are you writing this document?

- What do you want to say?

- How will your reader use your document?

- How should you organize the information?

- How should you present the information?

---

# 3. Make Your Writing Effective

After you've answered the questions about your readers and your document, summarize your findings in a few notes that you can refer to as you write. Keep in mind these key points:

- what the document is meant to do
- what your reader wants and needs to know
- what you need to say
- how you can organize the information

## Organize Your Ideas

Since your reader's needs are your main concern in organizing your text, ask yourself what your reader already knows and would most like to know. Put yourself in your reader's place. If you were he or she, what is the most important thing you would want to know? If you are not sure, find out before you start writing.

Put the most important ideas first in your document and in each paragraph. For example, you may have to list the dates when the five committees met to work on the research report over the past two years. But don't put this information at the beginning if your reader isn't likely to want to know it. Your reader may be more interested in knowing the dates when people will be invited to comment on the discussion paper. By putting that information in early, you will encourage your reader to read on.

# Help Your Reader Find Important Information

Use your introduction to tell your reader what your document is about and how it is organized. For longer documents, you may also need a table of contents. In the text, use headings to break up the information into manageable bits. Headings are easy for your reader to remember and use for quick reference later. By breaking up the text in this way, you make your document look less intimidating to the reader.

You may use working headings in your first draft and revise them later. Don't be surprised if you find it easier to decide on headings and write the introduction after you've drafted most of your document. Review your introduction when everything else is written, so that you can include changes in format or content.

# Write the Way You Speak

Use a conversational tone in your writing, address your reader personally and use examples that are meaningful to your reader's background and experience.

Written English is often much more formal than conversational English. While writing, imagine your reader is listening to you as you read your document aloud. You might find it difficult to actually say this sentence:

> This senior-level committee would be mandated to provide support to the Directorate in the establishment of a clear mandate of its role throughout the Department, with due consideration given to available person-years and financial resources.

The following version is closer to conversational English:

> This committee would help the Directorate develop
> a mandate that can be carried out with available staff
> and money.

# Address Your Readers Directly

Talk directly to your reader. Use the words **you, I, we, us** and
**our** to make your document more personal. Don't refer to
your reading audience in the third person, as **people, citizens,
clients, patients, consumers** or **customers**.

**Instead of:**

> The client can make application to the Department of
> Motor Vehicles for licensing before June 1.

**Use:**

> You can apply to the Department of Motor Vehicles
> for your licence before June 1.

Instead of addressing employers and students **directly**, one
government pamphlet talks **indirectly** about them:

> ...the program challenges employers from all sectors
> to create meaningful summer jobs that can give young
> people real learning opportunities. By responding
> to the challenge, employers in all sectors stand to
> strengthen the calibre of Canada's future workforce.

If rewritten, the pamphlet could speak to employers and use examples that are relevant to them. For example:

> Whether you run a car repair shop or manage a large financial company, you can give a young person a meaningful summer job. By giving a student an opportunity to learn about your business, you are helping to train Canada's future workforce.

The next example talks directly to students and uses examples that are relevant and meaningful to them.

> You can get a loan of up to $7,500 interest free for the first year of the five-year loan term....

> You must contribute some of your own assets to the operations, either cash or some equipment useful to the business: a car, tools, garage space, etc.

When you include examples to illustrate your point, you help your reader understand how the ideas might apply in real life.

## TO MAKE YOUR WRITING EFFECTIVE:

- organize your ideas

- put the most important ideas first

- help your reader find important information

- write the way you speak

- address your readers directly

# 4. Clear and Simple— Paragraphs and Sentences

Plain language writing emphasizes clarity. With plain language techniques you can get your reader interested, highlight your most important information and make sure that your message is delivered in the most effective way possible. *Clear* and *simple* are the goals for paragraphs and sentences to make sure you say what you really mean.

## Limit Each Paragraph to One Idea

Limit each paragraph to one idea unless you are linking related points. If you are comparing the old and the new, for example, it makes sense to bring them together in one paragraph. But make sure that the ideas are easily understood. Complicated information, or a discussion of several different ideas, generally needs to be broken up into separate paragraphs to be easily understood.

The following summary on tariffs was meant to explain a complicated issue in a simple way:

> The tariff has been an important but waning import policy instrument in Canada for many decades. More than 75 per cent of Canada–United States trade now moves free of duty. This figure, however, fails to take account

of the trade which could take place but for tariffs. High U.S. tariffs... continue to pose serious barriers to the U.S. market and prevent Canadian firms from achieving the economies of scale on which increased competitiveness and employment in Canadian industry depend...

This paragraph continues, including a sample listing of tariffs and still more information! It is very difficult for most readers to make the link quickly from a general statement about tariffs, to the current use of tariffs, to the secondary market effects of tariffs, to the effect of tariffs on competitiveness and employment, to...

The information can be re-organized and explained more fully using separate paragraphs. For example:

The tariff, a tax on imported goods, has been an important element of Canada's import policy for many decades. Its use has declined over the years, however, so that today more than three-quarters of Canada–U.S. trade moves free of duty.

It may be in Canada's best interest to eliminate more tariffs. High U.S. tariffs are barriers to Canadian firms entering the U.S. market. If these barriers did not exist, Canadian trade with the United States would probably increase.

With access to the U.S. market, Canadian firms could achieve economies of scale in their production. This is critical to our competitiveness and to employment in Canadian industry.

# Don't Overload Sentences

Don't place a new idea in the middle of a sentence. If you have a related point you want to make, use another sentence. If you want to give some details, use another paragraph. Don't cram information into one sentence. For example:

> However, by virtue of subsection 32(3) of the PSEA, an employee may apply to the Department for leave of absence (without pay) to seek political office (in a federal, provincial or territorial election) and the employee may be granted leave if the Department is of the opinion that the usefulness to the Public Service of the employee in the position he then occupies would not be impaired by reason of his having been a candidate for election...

The above example could be improved in a number of ways:

- the ideas it contains can be broken up into separate sentences
- the writer could have addressed "you" directly

For example:

> However, under section 32(3) of the PSEA, you can apply to the Department for a leave of absence without pay to run for office in a federal, provincial or territorial election. The Department may grant you leave if it finds that your ability to work in your current job will not be impaired because of your candidacy.

# Active Sentences

Your sentences should use a conversational tone. They should be:

- simply constructed
- limited to one idea
- positive in tone

In the active voice, the subject of a sentence is the doer of the action. Follow the usual word order in your sentences — subject, verb, object. This helps make sure you use the active voice. Your sentences will be easier to understand.

Many government documents use the passive voice, which can sound very impersonal.

**Instead of:**

> In early April, all applications will be reviewed by the committee.

**Use:**

> The committee will review all applications in early April.

Since it is the committee that is doing the action, why not mention it first?

There are times when the passive voice is useful, usually when the subject is not important or you don't know the subject.

**For example:**

> A number of programming options were tried throughout the '80s.

Put the subject and verb close to the beginning of the sentence. Too much information between the subject and the verb makes it difficult for the reader to find out what the subject of the sentence is doing.

**Instead of:**

> The committee, which was assembled at the request of the Cabinet on the recommendation of the coalition of citizens' groups, will consider alternative approaches.

**Use:**

> The coalition of citizens' groups recommended that Cabinet assemble the committee. At the Cabinet's request, the committee will consider alternative approaches to...

Don't change well-known phrases or expressions because they seem to go against a grammar rule or some other convention. You can end a sentence with a preposition if the phrasing sounds natural. Sir Winston Churchill once commented on writing which he felt was bureaucratic by saying:

> "This is the sort of English up with which I will not put."

Don't be afraid to start sentences with **and, or, but, for, so** or **yet**. It is an easy way to shorten long sentences.

**Instead of:**

> We had expected to meet our participation targets, but increased workloads because of the introduction of new programs kept us from travelling to northern locations as frequently as we had planned.

**Use:**

> We had expected to meet our participation targets. But, with new programs, our workload increased and we couldn't travel to northern locations as frequently as we had planned.

# Keep It Short

Readers can only take in so much new information at one time. So some people recommend that sentences should average about 15 words in length and that no sentence should be more than 25 words long. This rule is not hard-and-fast, however. A variety of sentence lengths can add interest to your writing. Readers can understand longer sentences if they are well-constructed and use familiar terms. Clear is best.

**Instead of:**

> This policy does not appear to be well understood by line management in the Region, even though this group has a primary responsibility for implementing the policy.

**Use:**

> The regional managers who are most responsible for carrying out this policy do not seem to understand it well.

Shorter is better.

# Keep It Simple

The following sentence, on the other hand, could use some additional explanation.

**Instead of:**

> Plateauing or career blockage refers to structural barriers to career advancement arising due to a combination of age imbalances and a static or contracting workforce.

**Use:**

> "Plateauing" or "career blockage" refers to the lack of opportunities for public servants to be promoted to the executive level. This problem arises because there is a large number of public servants who may have many years to work before they retire and because the size of the public service is being reduced. For these reasons, there are fewer openings available at higher levels.

As you can see, the sentence on plateauing needed a lot more explanation to be understood by most readers.

It took a paragraph of 63 words to better explain the terms clearly. Shorter isn't always best. Which of the two paragraphs would you rather read?

When you have a lot of information on one subject, break up long sentences by using point form to list important elements. But keep the lists short and group similar points together. For example, instead of making one list of a meeting's objectives, divide the list into objectives on information-sharing, decisions needed, follow-up action and so on.

Another way to break up blocks of information and draw the reader's attention to important elements is to use a question-and-answer format. In a government publication written for teenagers, the following sequence of section headings was used to help young people find the information important to them:

- What happens when you are arrested?
- What happens in court if you are between twelve and seventeen?
- What happens in court if you are eighteen and over?

Be careful using charts and graphics to explain information. People with poor math skills can find charts hard to understand. When using graphics, you must be sure that the images mean the same thing to your reader as they do to you. Test the graphics with people who would be likely to read your document. Make sure graphics work for you, not against you.

# Link Your Ideas

Don't shorten sentences by leaving out words such as **that**, **which** and **who**. Use these words to link the ideas in a sentence and make the meaning clearer for your reader.

The following sentence, without its connecting words, is far from clear.

> The driver of the truck passing by told the officer in the cruiser the car he saw hit the little girl in the intersection was red.

What or who was red? The car? The girl? The light? How many vehicles were involved in the accident?

The sentence could be rewritten as follows:

> The driver of the truck told the officer in the cruiser that, as he was passing by, he saw a red car hit the little girl in the intersection.

# Avoid Ambiguity

**Proper words in proper places make the true definition of style.**

*Swift*

When a pronoun is used, there should be no doubt as to which noun it represents.

**Instead of:**

> Michelle researched and wrote the speech herself, which everyone thought was impressive.

**Use:**

> Everyone was impressed with the speech that Michelle researched and wrote herself.

Adverbs and adverbial phrases also need to be placed properly to avoid confusion. If improperly placed, the adverbs **only, even, both, merely, just, also, mainly, in particular** and **at least** can cause confusion.

**Instead of:**

> Supervisors and staff are required to both participate in orientation sessions and department seminars.

**Use:**

> Supervisors and staff are required to participate both in orientation sessions and in departmental seminars.

# Emphasize the Positive

Positive sentences are inviting and encourage people to read on. Negative sentences can seem bossy or hostile. They don't encourage people to read on. People are generally more receptive to positive messages.

**Instead of:**

> If you fail to pass the examination, you will not qualify for admission.

**Use:**

> You must pass the examination to qualify for admission.

Use negative phrasing to emphasize danger, legal pitfalls or other warnings. It is also appropriate to use negative phrasing to allay fears or dispel myths. For example, a federal AIDS brochure first asks:

> How does HIV spread?

After that has been explained, the writers answer the question:

> How is HIV not spread?
>
> The virus is not spread through casual everyday contact. In the workplace this includes shaking hands, sharing work equipment, cutlery, coffee mugs or glasses. Washrooms and water fountains can also be shared without risk of HIV infection.

# Avoid Double Negatives

It isn't quite enough to remember that a double negative makes a positive. We avoid writing "I don't know nothing about it" if we mean that we know nothing about it. But watch out for two or more negative constructions in a sentence.

**Instead of:**

- He was not absent.
- The procedure will not be ineffective.
- It was never illegitimate.

**Use:**

- He was present.
- The procedure will be effective.
- It was always legitimate.

## THINK ABOUT YOUR CHOICE OF PARAGRAPHS AND SENTENCES:

- limit each paragraph to one idea
- don't overload sentences
- use active sentences
- keep sentences and paragraphs short
- keep sentences simple
- link your ideas
- avoid ambiguity in your sentences
- emphasize the positive
- avoid double negatives

# 5. Think about Your Choice of Words

Plain language writing emphasizes the use of the clearest words possible to describe actions, objects and people. That often means choosing a two-syllable word over a three-syllable one, an old, familiar term instead of the latest bureaucratic expression, and sometimes, several clear words instead of one complicated word.

As with all the other elements of plain language writing, your choice of words should be based on what will be clearer for your reader. If you're not sure, ask. Test out your document with some of the people who are likely to use it. To help you draft easy-to-understand documents, here are some guidelines on your choice of words.

## Use Simple, Everyday Words

> **Get to the point as directly as you can; never use a big word if a little one will do.**
>
> *Emily Carr*

Use simple, familiar words instead of unfamiliar words.

Plain language writing involves expressing yourself the way you speak. When you talk to someone, you make an effort to be understood. So when you write, imagine that someone is asking you what you mean. Explain your idea using clear and familiar words. Here are a few examples of simple words and phrases you might substitute for less familiar or multi-syllable words:

| Instead of: | Use: |
|---|---|
| accomplish | do |
| ascertain | find out |
| disseminate | send out, distribute |
| endeavour | try |
| expedite | hasten, speed up |
| facilitate | make easier, help |
| formulate | work out, devise, form |
| in lieu of | instead of |
| locality | place |
| optimum | best, greatest, most |
| strategize | plan |
| utilize | use |

# Cut Out Unnecessary Words

Cut out unnecessary words or replace a group of words with one word to make your writing clearer. Here is a sample list of some alternative words for common, wordy expressions:

| Instead of: | Use: |
|---|---|
| with regard to | about |
| by means of | by |
| in the event that | if |
| until such time | until |
| during such time | while |
| in respect of | for |
| in view of the fact | because |
| on the part of | by |
| subsequent to | after |
| under the provisions of | under |
| with a view to | to |
| it would appear that | apparently |
| it is probable that | probably |
| notwithstanding the fact that | although |
| adequate number of | enough |
| excessive number of | too many |

# Avoid Using Jargon

> If language is not correct, then what is said is not what is meant; if what is said is not what is meant, then what ought to be done remains undone.
>
> *Confucius*

Government workers are familiar with many forms of government jargon. However, using jargon can create problems because the public may not understand it. Don't use a term such as "vertical federalism" in a paper that may be distributed to the public unless you explain it clearly in the text. But if you have to explain a term, why not use an alternate expression from the start?

**Instead of:**

> The perceived acceptability of disparities caused by differences in preferences is based on allocative efficiency.

**Use:**

> People see unequal service as fair if they are getting what they want.

Trendy, fashionable expressions, such as "level playing field", "downtime", "leading edge", "streamline", "interface with" and "rationalization of resources" are used far too often. They can undermine the impact of what you're trying to say because they are not well understood by the public. The fact that they are trendy will also mean that they will soon date your writing. Avoid them.

**Instead of:**

> You will receive reactivation and assistance consistent with your requirements.

**Use:**

> You will get the amount of help you need.

# Avoid or Explain Technical Words

Avoid technical words or explain them on the same page
where they appear in the text.

**Instead of:**

> These factors have contributed to a more bimodal
> distribution of earnings.

**Use:**

> These factors help make the rich richer and the poor
> poorer.

**Instead of:**

> If you see a crime committed, you may receive a
> subpoena.

**Use:**

> If you see a crime committed, you may receive a
> "subpoena." A subpoena is an order of the court
> telling you when and where you must appear to testify
> as a witness in a trial.

Glossaries (list and explanation of terms) are more difficult to
use if they are placed at the end of a book or booklet. If you
prefer to define technical terms outside the text, try placing a
box defining the words on the same page.

# Don't Change Verbs into Nouns

Nouns created from verbs usually give a sentence an impersonal tone. They are harder for the reader to understand.

**Instead of:**

> The **requirement** of the Department is that employees work seven and one-half hours a day.

**Use:**

> The Department **requires** employees to work seven and one-half hours a day.

**Instead of:**

> The **implementation** of the rule necessitated a **reassessment** of policy.

**Use:**

> When the Directorate **put the rule into practice**, the Department **had to reassess** its policy.

# Avoid Chains of Nouns

Chains of nouns are strings of two or more nouns used to name one thing. They are often difficult for a reader to understand, and give a bureaucratic tone to documents. You may have encountered such burdensome expressions as:

- resource allocation procedures
- transport facility development programming
- consumer information-seeking behaviour
- product extension mergers

Noun chains take some effort to untangle. They lack connecting words, such as **of, for, about, in** and the possessive marker, **'s**, that would clarify how the nouns relate to each other.

**Instead of:**

> World population is increasing faster than world food production.

**Use:**

> The world's population is increasing faster than its food production.

# Explain Complex Ideas

If you are talking about research, policies or programs, don't dwell on the theory at the expense of practical descriptions. It may be important to tell people what your research goals were and how your findings have validated your working hypothesis. But you should be careful to define all the technical terms and give concrete examples of what you mean.

Complicated ideas need special attention. For example, you may believe that your reader understands what you mean by "bona fide occupational requirement." But it is important to explain complex terms anyway. Help your reader out. The following text contains a number of complex ideas:

> Expansion of existing services beyond the initial capitalization would be based on demonstrated market need and a record of cost-effective delivery. Funding of expansion up to a level sufficient to sustain the integrity of the capital base with good management will be by non-repayable contribution.

What type of expansion? What kind of services? What is initial capitalization? How is demonstrated market need assessed? The reader needs a solid background in several subjects to wade through this text. Explain your terms from the start or your reader may not read on.

In the following text, a complicated theoretical term is defined in a concrete way:

> The consumer price index measures monthly and yearly changes in the cost of 300 goods and services

commonly bought by Canadians. If the combined cost of this "basket" of items goes up, then there has been inflation. The greater the increase, the higher the inflation rate has become.

# Choose Your Words Carefully

Be consistent in what you call something. Avoid using two or more names for the same thing. Variation for its own sake can confuse the reader.

Do not be afraid to repeat the same word or the same idea if it is important. For example, it may be important for a person to keep a record of each step taken in applying for a grant. It makes sense to repeat that idea several times in documents about the application process.

# Use Acronyms Carefully

Acronyms are formed from the first letter of the words which they represent. Remember that not everyone will know the organization or program that the letters refer to. Not everyone knows that "SIN" refers to "Social Insurance Number." Put the acronym in brackets the first time you use the proper term. Then you can use the acronym in the rest of your text.

Some acronyms, such as U.S.A. or R.C.M.P., may be so well-known that they need no explanation and may be written with or without periods after each letter. Ask yourself whether your reader is likely to know the acronym you want to use. When in doubt, spell it out.

## THINK ABOUT YOUR CHOICE OF WORDS:

- use simple, everyday words
- cut out unnecessary words
- avoid jargon
- avoid or explain technical words
- don't change verbs into nouns
- avoid chains of nouns
- explain complex ideas
- choose your words carefully
- use acronyms carefully

# 6. Appearances Are Very Important

The way you present information on the page is just as important as the words and sentences you use to present that information. A well-written document is harder to read if it is poorly laid-out. A good format helps highlight important information, links related sections and separates others. How your document looks can make the difference between your message being understood or lost.

## Spacing

Pages of long paragraphs without lists or summaries appear harder to read than they need to.

- Keep your paragraphs short, generally no more than four or five sentences.
- Leave space between paragraphs.
- Divide your document into sections of related information.
- Don't print on every inch of space on your page. For example, if you are using a column format, use only two columns for your text on a three-column page. Part of the extra white space can be used to draw attention to important information in boxes or boldface type.
- Be generous with margin space.

Do not use right justification. Use unjustified or ragged right-hand margins. When text is printed with a justified right margin, the letters or words on longer lines are spaced closer together, while letters or words on shorter lines are spread further apart, to even out the lines. Constantly adjusting to these changes is tiring to the eyes. Right justification can produce a lot of hyphenated words, which present another reading challenge.

Compare these texts:

| RIGHT JUSTIFICATION | RAGGED RIGHT MARGIN |
|---|---|
| Technology, like international competition and the emergence of an integrated world economy, is changing the way Canadians work. Computers are familiar pieces of equipment in offices and factories, and Canadians working on the shop floor and in the boardroom are having to learn new tasks. The new workplace skills require more education, more training, better communication, higher levels of literacy. Skilled minds are taking over from the skilled hands of yesteryear. | Technology, like international competition and the emergence of an integrated world economy, is changing the way Canadians work. Computers are familiar pieces of equipment in offices and factories, and Canadians working on the shop floor and in the boardroom are having to learn new tasks. The new workplace skills require more education, more training, better communication, higher levels of literacy. Skilled minds are taking over from the skilled hands of yesteryear. |

# Headings and Sub-Headings

If you use clear headings and sub-headings, the reader will be able to find specific information in your document. Some sample headings that can capture your reader's attention are:

- How can I get help right away?
- What is a preliminary inquiry?
- What you can do
- Where to find answers and information on drugs

# Highlighting

Use boxes to separate key information from the rest of your text. The information will stand out more on the page.

Highlight headings, words or phrases with boldface type, but don't overuse it. If only a few words or phrases are highlighted, the reader will notice them even when just glancing at the page.

Other types of highlighting are:

- Bullets — Use them for point-form lists and summaries. They can be stylized as arrows or miniature graphics.
- Italic print — Use it to emphasize a phrase or word, as in, "I told him he could do the project, but on *his* time!" Italics are also used for phrases in other languages. Don't overuse italic print. In large amounts, it is difficult to read.
- Underlining — Use it under titles or to add emphasis.
- Colour — Use it to add interest to the page, if your budget permits. Shaded areas can also be used to set text apart.

# Table of Contents

Make a table of contents for long documents. It tells readers something about the organization of your document and makes it easy to find information. Although this is useful to all readers, it is especially important for people with low reading skills, who cannot skim through your document quickly and easily.

You can use questions, phrases, names or short descriptions as section or chapter titles, such as:

- The New Job Market
- Self-Help    — What Is It?
                      — Where Do I Find a Group?

# Type Style and Size

Choose a solid, plain typeface which is easy to read.

Don't combine many different typefaces on the same page, because it will give a very busy, confusing appearance. Different typefaces should be used consistently, but only occasionally, for emphasis or to set some information apart.

Make sure the type size is big enough for your readers. People will often skip over text which is too small. Small type makes a document look crammed and uninviting. A ten point type size is a good minimum size to use. Be sure to consider that seniors, people with visual impairment and others prefer a larger type size.

- Don't use capital letters to emphasize large blocks of text. In ALL CAPS, all word shapes are rectangular and less familiar to the reader. In upper and lower case, words have distinct shapes that are more easily recognized. Text in ALL CAPS is harder to read, especially for more than a few words, as this example shows:

> TEXT SET IN ALL-CAPITALS IS HARDER TO READ THAN TEXT SET IN UPPER AND LOWER CASE. RESEARCHERS HAVE FOUND THAT PEOPLE READ CONTINUOUS CAPITAL LETTERS AT A SLOWER RATE THAN SMALL LETTERS.

- ALL CAPS can be useful to draw attention to headings or a brief statement, such as:

**PLEASE PRINT**

- The type size of headings should be noticeably larger than the text.

- A serif typeface, with hooks on each letter, makes text easier to read because it leads your eye from letter to letter. A sans serif typeface, which has no hooks on letters, can be good for titles. It leads your eye down into the body of the text. This guide uses a serif typeface for the text, and a sans serif typeface for the headings.

# Colour of Ink and Paper

- Use a dark ink, such as navy blue or black, on light paper — white or cream, for example.

- Avoid colour combinations with low contrast, such as blue with green, or pink or yellow on white.

- Avoid large passages of light print on black background.

# Graphics and Illustrations

You can add interest to your document with illustrations, photographs, diagrams, lines and symbols. However, use graphics with caution. Make sure that they mean the same thing to your reader as they do to you. Ask people who would be using your document to look over your choice of graphics and illustrations. Are the symbols easily recognizable? Do the lines help guide the reader? Don't overuse graphics.

Tables, charts and graphs can be useful for anyone familiar with them. However, these visual aids are generally more difficult to use and understand and you cannot assume that people will understand them. So make sure you are using graphics and illustrations that are appropriate for your reading audience.

The right kind of visual aids can help your reader understand your message and remember what you have written. Place all graphics and illustrations as close as possible to the text they refer to.

## THINK ABOUT THE APPEARANCE OF YOUR DOCUMENT:

- spacing
- headings and sub-headings
- highlighting
- table of contents
- type style and size
- colour of ink and paper
- graphics and illustrations

# 7. Check with the Experts—Your Readers

It is important to get feedback from people who are likely to use your document. We often write documents which are more suitable for ourselves than for our readers.

Try field testing your document. Ask several of the people whom you expect to read the document to assess its value. Ask them if it is something they would enjoy reading, if they would indeed read it and if it all makes sense to them. Once you have incorporated their comments, test your document with a larger group. The time and effort spent field testing is worth the effort. Only your readers can tell you if your writing is useful, relevant and readable. Chapter 9, **For More Information**, provides a list of resources which may assist you with field testing and focus group testing.

If you use a personal computer to write, you may wish to use available grammar and style software packages to ensure that you have followed grammar rules. These grammar check programs can help you spot writing errors such as

- incomplete sentences
- passive voice
- jargon
- long sentences
- negative sentences

They can suggest changes to correct these problems. The programs can also provide you with an approximate reading level for your writing. They can tell you, for example, if your text is accessible to people at the grade eight or grade eighteen level. A high score usually means that a document is not easily understandable.

However, use readability indexes and computer programs as guides and handy tools. Don't use them as the final assessment of your writing. Ultimately, the reader is the best judge of whether or not your document is easily understood. Only people can give you truly expert views.

## TO BE SURE YOU'RE WRITING PLAIN LANGUAGE:

- check with the experts — your readers

- field test

- ask someone else to read your draft

- use available grammar and style software packages as guides only

# 8. A Check List

This list provides you with a guide to help you gauge your success in writing plainly. It summarizes the key concepts presented in the guide.

**1.    Reading Audience**

- Who is likely to read this document?
- What is the best format for this message to this audience?

**2.    Purpose**

- Why are you writing it?
- What do you want to say?
- Have you included the most important information?

**3.    Organization**

- Have you based the order of your material on the reader's needs?
- Does the important information come first?
- Have you said what you have to say, and no more?

**4.    Tone**

- Have you considered your reader's needs and written to the reader directly?
- Do you sound helpful, appropriately personal?
- Does your text read like informal conversation?

## 5. Style

- Have you limited the length of your paragraphs?
- Are your sentences short and clear?
- Have you used familiar words, consistent terms and concrete examples?

## 6. Design

- Is your design attractive and easy to read, with lots of white space and breaks in the text?
- Have you helped people find the information they need? Are the book's contents described in your introduction? Have you included a table of contents?
- Can the reader understand your graphics and illustrations?
- Do the graphics and illustrations help your text?

## 7. Checking with Your Reading Audience

- Have you asked a sample group of readers to check your draft document?

# 9. For More Information

## Plain Language — General

Bailey, Edward, P. Jr. *Writing Clearly: A Contemporary Approach.* Columbus: Charles E. Merrill Publishing Company, 1984.

Baldwin, Ruth. *Clear Writing and Literacy.* Prepared for the Ontario Literacy Coalition. Toronto: 1990.

Bates, Jefferson D. *Writing with Precision: How to Write So That You Cannot Possibly Be Misunderstood; Zero Base Gobbledygook.* Washington: Acropolis Books, 1980.

Birchfield, Martha J. *The Plain Language Movement: Away from Legalese and Federalese: A Bibliography.* Monticello, Illinois: Vance Bibliographies, 1986.

Canadian Bar Association and the Canadian Bankers' Association. *The Decline and Fall of Gobbledygook: Report on Plain Language Documentation.* Toronto: 1990.

Collins, C. Edward and Hugh Read. *Plain English: A Guide to Standard Usage and Clear Writing.* Scarborough: Prentice-Hall, 1989.

Cutts, Martin, and Chrissie Maher. *Gobbledygook.* London, England: George Allen & Unwin, 1984.

Cutts, Martin, and Chrissie Maher. *The Plain English Story.* Stockport, England: Plain English Campaign, 1986.

Dorney, Jacqueline M. *The Plain English Movement.* ERIC Clearinghouse on Reading and Communication Skills. Washington: Office of Education Research and Improvement (ERIC), 1987.

Dowis, Richard. *How to Make Your Writing Reader-Friendly.* White Hall, Virginia: Betterway Publications, 1990.

Eagleson, Robert D. *The Case for Plain Language.* Toronto: Plain Language Centre, Canadian Legal Information Centre, 1989.

Einstein, Charles. *How to Communicate: The Manning, Selvage and Lee Guide to Clear Writing and Speech.* New York: McGraw-Hill, 1985.

Flesch, Rudolf. *How to Write Plain English: A Book for Lawyers and Consumers.* New York: Harper & Row, 1979.

Gowers, Sir Ernest. *The Complete Plain Words.* Harmondsworth: Penguin Books, 1987.

Gray, Lee L. *Journal of Studies in Technical Careers.* V. 9, no. 1, pp 17–19, Wisconsin, 1987.

Health and Welfare Canada, Seniors Secretariat. *Communicating in Print With/About Seniors.* Ottawa: Supply and Services Canada, 1991.

Lutz, William. *Doublespeak: From "Revenue Enhancement" to "Terminal Living" — How Government, Business, Advertisers, and Others Use Language to Deceive You.* New York: Harper & Row, 1989.

Nore, Gordon W.E. *Clear Lines.* Toronto: Frontier College, 1991.

Redish, Janice C. *The Language of Bureaucracy.* Paper presented at the Conference on Literacy in the 1980's, Ann Arbor, Michigan, June 24–27, 1981. Washington: American Institute for Research in the Behavioral Sciences, 1981.

Saskatchewan Consumer and Commercial Affairs. *Plain Language for the Saskatchewan Government — Policy and Guidelines.* 1991.

Steinberg, Erwin Ray (ed.). P*lain Language: Principles and Practice.* Detroit: Wayne State University Press, 1991.

Vernon, Tom. *Gobbledegook.* London: National Consumer Council Pamphlet Series, no. 756, 1980.

# Design

Felker, D.B. (ed.). *Guidelines for Document Designers.* Washington, D.C.: American Institute for Research, 1981.

# Newsletters

*Clarity.* The Plain Language Centre Newsletter. Canadian Legal Information Centre, 600 Eglinton Avenue East, Suite 205, Toronto, Ontario M4P 1P3

*PROSEBUST!* Prosebusters! a division of B&B Editorial Consulting Ltd., 563 Gladstone Avenue, Ottawa, Ontario K1R 5P2

# Workshops

Baldwin, Ruth. *Plain Writing Services*, P.O. Box 6086, Station J, Ottawa, Ontario K2A 1T1 (613-726-0553)
* workshops on plain writing

Breen, Mary J. *Clear Language Consultant,* 309 Engleburn Avenue, Peterborough, Ontario K9H 1S8 (705-745-3891)
* workshops in clear writing for community groups and health care workers

Davies, Gwen. *Davies Communications Consulting,* 6152 Duncan Street, Halifax, Nova Scotia B3L lK2 (902-423-7707)
* workshops for community groups, public servants, health care professionals and members of the legal community

Frontier College, *Learning in the Workplace*, 35 Jackes Avenue, Toronto, Ontario M4T lE2 (416-923-3591)
* workshops on clear language writing and document design

Grotsky, Rose. *Learning Communications Inc.*, 561 Markham Street, Toronto, Ontario M6G 2L6 (416-588-4646)
* workshops on plain writing and document design for government (federal/provincial/municipal levels) and the private sector

Mindach, Chuck. *Business Forms Management Association, Inc.* (BFMA), 103 du Geai-Bleu, Hull, Quebec J9A 1W4 (819-956-3145)
* Drafting documents in plain language
* Plain language forms analysis and design

Mowat, Christine. *Wordsmith Associates,* 436 Silver Valley Drive NW, Calgary, Alberta T3B 4C2 (403-286-6865)
- business writing for professionals, tailored to a specific organization

*Prosebusters!* a division of B&B Editorial Consulting Ltd., 563 Gladstone Avenue, Ottawa, Ontario K1R 5P2
- seminar on effective writing

*Straight Talk Institute,* 2975–700 W. Georgia, P.O. Box 10074, Vancouver, B.C. V7Y 1B6 (604-681-1062)
- workshops for government agencies and industry

Vale, Mark. *The Plain Language Centre,* Canadian Legal Information Centre (CLIC), 600 Eglinton Ave. E., Suite 205, Toronto, Ontario M4P 1P3 (416-483-3802)
- workshops in use of plain language
- workshops for people who do in-house training in plain language
- workshops in public testing of documents

# Resources

Baldwin, Ruth. *Plain Writing Services,* P.O. Box 6086, Station J., Ottawa, Ontario, K2A 1T1 (613-726-0553)

Breen, Mary J. *Clear Language Consultant,* 309 Engleburn Avenue, Peterborough, Ontario K9H 1S8 (705-745-3891)

Catano, Janice. *Plain Language and Health Consultant,* 6246 Shirley Street, Halifax, Nova Scotia B3H 2N6 (902-422-6123)

Davies, Gwen. *Davies Communications Consulting,* 6152 Duncan Street, Halifax, Nova Scotia B3L 1K2 (902-423-7707)

Frontier College, *Learning in the Workplace,* 35 Jackes Avenue, Toronto, Ontario M4T 1E2 (416-923-3591)

Godin, Joanne. *Consulting Writer,* 918 Alenmede Crescent, Ottawa, Ontario K2B 8K5 (613-237-4097)

Grotsky, Rose. *Learning Communications Inc.,* 561 Markham Street, Toronto, Ontario M6G 2L6 (416-588-4646)

Horwood, Lorne. *Plain Language Resource Centre,* NGL Consulting Ltd., 280 Albert Street, Ottawa, Ontario K1P 5G8 (613-236-5850)

James, Margaret. *Plain Language Project,* Continuing Legal Education Society of B.C., 150–900 Howe Street, Vancouver, B.C. V6Z 2M4 (604-669-3546)

Knight, Phil. *Plain Language Institute of B.C.,* 1500–555 W. Hastings, Vancouver, B.C. V6B 4N6 (604-687-8895)

Lipsett, Lori. *Clear Language Committee,* Saskatchewan Public Service Commission, Room 401, 2103–11th Avenue, Regina, Saskatchewan S4P 3V7 (306-787-7555)

Lloyd, Betty-Ann. *Kaleidoscope Communications,* 5533 Black Street, Halifax, Nova Scotia B3K 1P7 (902-455-0185)

Mowat, Christine. *Wordsmith Associates,* 436 Silver Valley Drive NW, Calgary, Alberta T3B 4C2 (403-286-6865)

*Ontario Literacy Coalition,* Clear Language Committee, 365 Bloor Street East, Suite 1003, Toronto, Ontario M4W 3L4 (416-963-5787)

*Prosebusters!* a division of B&B Editorial Consulting Ltd., 563 Gladstone Ave., Ottawa, Ontario K1R 5P2 (613-594-5555)

*Straight Talk Institute,* 2975–700 W. Georgia, P.O. Box 10074, Vancouver, B.C. V7Y 1B6 (604-681-1062)

Vale Mark. *The Plain Language Centre,* Canadian Legal Information Centre (CLIC), 600 Eglinton Ave. E., Suite 205, Toronto, Ontario M4P 1P3 (416-483-3802)

**Note:** This chapter "For More Information" is not intended to be an endorsement of specific individuals or companies. It contains the best information on resources available at the time of printing.

# THANKS

We want to thank a number of individuals and organizations whose work inspired ours:

- Ruth Baldwin, Plain Writing Services
- Jacqueline Bossé-Andrieu, University of Ottawa
- Mary J. Breen, Clear Language Consultant
- Canadian Bar Association and Canadian Bankers' Association, *The Decline and Fall of Gobbledygook: Report on Plain Language Documentation*
- Marie-Luce Constant, Littris
- Bernard Deschênes, Trans-Script
- Joanne Godin, Consulting Writer
- Stan Jones, Carleton University
- Phil Knight, B.C. Plain Language Institute
- Penny Lawler and Barbara Shields, Literacy Branch, Ontario Ministry of Education
- Gillian McCreary, Government of Saskatchewan
- Gordon Norc, Frontier College
- *Prosebusters!* a division of B&B Editorial Consulting Ltd.
- Ceta Ramkhalawansing, City of Toronto
- Mark Vale, The Plain Language Centre, Canadian Legal Information Centre (CLIC)

Made in the USA
San Bernardino, CA
10 May 2017